POEMS FROM THE HEART

RADHAA PUBLISHING HOUSE

Copyright © 2024 by Radhaa Publishing House

All rights reserved.

No part of this book may be reproduced in any form or by any electronic or mechanical means, including information storage and retrieval systems, without written permission from the author, except for the use of brief quotations in a book review.

Foreword

"Poems From the Heart" is more than just an anthology; it is a tapestry woven with the threads of human experience, emotion, and connection. Curating this collection has been a profound journey, one that has brought together voices from across the globe— from the sun-kissed shores of the Philippines to the mystical landscapes of Iceland, from the historic streets of Portugal, Sweden to the vast expanses of Canada, from the rolling hills of England to the vibrant cities of Australia, and Spain, and from the diverse landscapes of the USA to the myriad places in: Los Angeles California, Florida, North Carolina, Oregon, New Mexico, New Hampshire, New Orleans, Minnesota, etc. where poets come together and collaborated on this beautiful book.

When we embarked on this journey, our vision was clear: to create a space where poets from diverse backgrounds could share their unique perspectives and touch the hearts of readers worldwide. Each poem in this anthology is a testament to the power of words, the universality of human emotions, and the beauty of our shared humanity.

As I reached out to poets across continents, I was continually amazed by the richness of their experiences and the depth of their insights. Despite the geographical distances, there was a common thread that bound us all—a profound desire to express our innermost thoughts and feelings, to connect with others on a deeply human level.

The poets featured in "Poems From the Heart" come from various walks of life, bringing with them their own cultural backgrounds, personal histories, and poetic styles. Yet, within the pages of this anthology, their voices converge to create a harmonious symphony of love, life, tragedy, loss, hope, and resilience. This collection is a celebration of timeless diversity, but also a reminder of our shared human experience.

Curating this anthology has also been a deeply personal journey for me. It has been a privilege to witness the vulnerability and bravery of each poet as they lay bare their hearts on these pages. Their words have moved me, challenged me, and inspired me. I hope that as you read through this collection, you too will be touched by the raw emotion and profound wisdom contained within these poems. Each Poem is a sovereign experience to express itself. And we are here to share with you these poems.

In a world that often feels fragmented and divided, "Poems From the Heart" serves as a beacon of unity and understanding. It is a reminder that, despite our differences, we are all connected by the same fundamental human experiences. Through the power of poetry, we can transcend borders and boundaries, and find solace and connection in the shared language of the heart.

Thank you for joining us on this journey. May these poems resonate with you, bring you comfort, and remind you of the beauty and resilience of the human spirit.

With heartfelt gratitude,
    Radhaa Nilia
    Founder of Radhaa Publishing House

Contents

1. POET: Queen Helen Abdurajak — 1
2. POET: Maya The Shaman — 6
3. POET: Christopher Seiffert — 16
4. POET: Patricia Wald-Hopkins — 22
5. POET: Deo Palma — 29
6. POET: Ebony Shalom xo — 33
7. POET: Neil Gaur — 42
8. POET: Caroline Roy (Care) — 52
9. POET: Sandra Basudde — 58
10. POET: Milallan Diipalii Younan — 61
11. POET: Radhaa Nilia — 75
12. POET: Diya Marie Miller — 87
13. POET: Joan of Angels — 90
14. POET: Cristal Ortiz — 93
15. POET: Wendy Ramirez — 96
16. POET: Lisa Littleton Samson — 98
17. POET: Dennis Freese — 104
18. POET: Alanna Starr Shimel — 115
19. POET: Hjalti Kristinsson — 119
20. POET: Leah Sonaria — 123
21. POET: Emmanuel Itier — 125
22. POET: Chrystina Box — 131
23. POET: Selma Harwell — 134
24. POET: Jessica Louise Phillips — 142
25. POET: Sabrina L. Avalo — 151
26. POET: Kari Russell — 153
27. POET: Aros Crystos — 155
28. POET: Blesilda Carmona De La Rosa — 157
29. ABOUT: Radhaa Publishing House — 159
30. Special Message to Our Readers — 165

POET: Queen Helen Abdurajak

I AM DIVINE WARRIOR

I am Ma. Helen Abdurajak, clad in divine armor
Endowed with courage and bravery so bright.
Fear and pain, those specters of the night
That banished by the light of my spiritual fight.

Though jealousy and darkness seek to claim
The divine gifts nestled within my soul's frame.
They falter, they stumble—they cannot tame
The spirit God guards with an eternal flame.

I stand before the world, a beacon so tall
Urging all to fight till the last breath does fall.

With self-determination, I heed the call
To save the just, the righteous, the all.

Join this crusade, let not fear nor doubt prevail
For this is not my journey alone
But a tale of all who guard their kin without fail
Who protect their homes through every gale.

We march to the rhythm of the final
battle's drum
Good against evil, the sum of all sums.
Side by side, with the light, we become
Warriors divine, under God's mighty thumb.

My mission is clear, my path is set
To free the poor from a gilded net.
Against cabals and powers, my stance is met
For the needy and the humble, my sun
does not set.

We are special creations, forged by divine hand
Walk with me through this blessed land—
From Mindanao's peaks to Sabah's sand
In Maharlika's fields, together we'll stand.

Defend, protect, uphold what is right
Our nation, our family, our people's plight.
In God's new kingdom, we'll find our light
Golden Age dawning, oh what a sight.

Guide the weak, lead them to day
On paths of light, where peace may lay.

In divine paradise, where joy may stay,
Where love rules hearts in a timeless sway.

Let there be peace on Earth, a chant, a creed
Forever and ever, as our spirits lead.
Amen.

MYSTICAL LEMURIA
By: *Queen Helen Abdurajak*

Long lived a mystical place
Lemuria, land of legends and magic
A place of Devoted chosen people
Where unique Divine paths connect

Ancestors descendants legacy
Exceptional abilities bestowed
Body entwined in profound mystery
Bearing spirit of ancestral ability

Devotees with supreme faith
Built on trust, truth and harmony
Masters of devotion and discipline
Inner self worth, faith and grace

Spiritual Self transcendence
Embarked the galactic journey
Enriched life full of mystery
Watchful eyes within my company

Every moment is a decision
To act with skillful intention
Evil eyes watch to find fault in me
Unable to catch a force, steadfast and free

A blessed chosen soul gifts bestowed

With brilliance divinely unmatched
Unbroken I stand eternally aligned
In vessel pure where sanctity reside

Lead by Creator, I shall walk with dignity
No one can ever blemish my integrity
Covered with my love and divinity
Lemurian I embark my chosen destiny

Unblemished in life's embrace
Unstoppable examples, by the chosen ones
I walk as beacon of peace and liberty
Where legents stand the test of time and harmony

POET: Maya The Shaman

POEM FROM "MY HEART"

In the realm of rhythm, where my life does start
A symphony of existence, titled
"Poem from My Heart."
I'll journey within, where verses impart
The tale of self love, my life-sustaining Heart.

In chambers unseen, my biological Art
Pumping life's essence, each beat a fresh start.
Scientific marvel, a work of fine chart
A rhythmic dance, a vital body part–My Heart.

Beyond my physical, my spiritual chart,
My Heart's whispers echo, my sacred Heart.

An expression profound, where my dreams impart, the canvas of desires, woven in my Heart.

In 3D Earth's embrace, where realities start,
My heartbeat resonates, a cosmic beat of my Heart. Connected dreams, like constellations that chart, My human purpose, from my soul to impart.

Harmony in humanity, a universal Art,
My Heart is a note, playing its part.
Love threads the fabric, a binding dart
Uniting my soul fragments—a transcendent Heart.

Gifted I am, with a creative spark,
My future contribution, a hopeful embark.
My heart's desires, a guiding mark,
A cosmic grid pulsating my celestial lark.

One breath, one task, in the cosmic arc
My journey unfolds, an ethereal spark.
Through my hearts beat, divine has touched
Back to the Creator, I surrender my majestic Heart.

LOLA SENYANG: MY BELOVED GRANDMOTHER
By: *Maya The Shaman*

Lola Senyang, my Father's Mother
She's my beloved dearest Grandmother
Born of pure Lemurian bloodline
Lived in Maharlika the land of promise

Lola Senyang and her sacred lineage
Told stories of her benevolent brave Father
Then her magical Lemurian grandfather
Don Pedro our cosmic great-great-grandfather

When evening comes
Lola Senyang stared at the flickering stars
As if waiting for something or someone
"Coming they will be," she said
At the right moment and time
Maybe in your lifetime, maybe not
But, whispered with endearing sweet voice
She said...

*"Long-long time ago,
The fall of Mu was foretold,
Time awaits, for Mu will rise again.
The rise of great ones will be known!
Angels born without their wings,
Rainbow warriors, at their best,*

*fearless and ready
to give their lives away,
for freedom they know
they seek the very best."*

Knowing there's more beyond their sight
They cast their love, strength and bright lights
When darkness falls they catch the many
Courage and Strength, made offerings so plenty

She said look at the skies
Angels in silver wings
One day they will arrive
To carry ancient future
promised made to all its people

Lola Senyang added
Keep your eyes peeled
for the Sacred Land of Mu.
Deep inside the Earth
and beyond the deep blue seas
Enchanted beings co-exist
Living in peace—mystery and harmony

The cosmic web of life expands
From etheric skies, surface lands
and under the green blue seas
Warriors of Light will rise again
To win this spiritual battle
Promised lands was meant to be
Free for both you and me!

DON PEDRO:
MY LEMURIAN GREAT-GREAT GRANDFATHER
By: *Maya The Shaman*

In my contemplative hours, when hope seems lost,
A beacon shone through the cosmic frost.
Don Pedro, my ancestor, from realms near and afar,
My Galactic Shamanic Guide, my celestial star.

He soared through skies and walks on waters,
Untouched by 3D realms' where low-life hovers.
No need for planes, land wheels, or ships
He travels through his Galactic ship.

Master of portals, dimensions wide,
On a "Bubble of Light," Don Pedro gracefully glide.
A traveller on cosmic realm, time and space
He shifted realms where dreams truly matter.

From 3D worlds to realms unseen,
He whispered truths in twilight's sheen.
"There are many like me," he'd softly say,
"Guardians of night, protectors of day."

From the Galactic void, he made his descent
To ancient Mu, where his journey was spent.
Lands now sunken, treasures deep hidden,
In the ocean's embrace, where secrets remain.

Beneath the waves, in blue-green light,
Coral reefs, vibrant and naturally bright.
Whales and dolphins, turtles so grand,
Guardians of this submerged Lemurian land.

Memories of Lemuria, fleeting and vast,
Echos through time, a shadow cast.
A kingdom lost, yet stories remain,
Whispered in dreams, in my heart's domain.

"Don Pedro," I called, in need of moments so fair
He answered, a presence, a breath of fresh air.
"You're never alone," he said with such grace,
"Your lineage lives in the cosmic space."

Through history's pages, tattered and torn,
In my DNA his essence remains.
He guides me still, through night and day,
My Great-great Galactic Shaman Grandfather,
"Don Pedro," is here to stay.

DESCENDANTS OF MU
By: *Maya The Shaman*

From Creator's sacred heart space
Descendants of Mu, arise and emerge
Never shall you forget your eternal sage
Celestial children of love, devotion so near.

Galactic threads in your essence spun
A cosmic mission beneath the stunning sun
From ancient realms, your journey begun
Angels in 3rd dimension, battles at hand.

Time's forgotten dreams kept in your souls
You'll never forget, remember your sacred role
With purpose divine, you reach your goals
Weaving heaven's tapestry, making it whole.

Across the globe, your presence pervade
Through trials and errors, you persist to hold
From distant shores to untrodden lands
Lemurian kin, guided by cosmic hands.

Bound by vows to the cosmic dance
Threads of lifetimes, in celestial trance
In cosmic mysteries, you take your chance
Written in stars, your sacred romance.

Earth's ancient guardians, tested and true

Never faltering, always seeing through
Blessed by the Source, in all you do
Aware of cycles, both old and new.

In your hearts lives the sacred heart's fire
Hold space for your deepest desire
Amidst Earth's changes, you never tire
Ready for the dawn of the cosmic choir.

Through ages past, through trials untold
Harmony's promise, a story behold
Now ready for service, brave and bold
In cosmic alignment, a tale has been told.

With hands outstretched, embracing the light
Ascension beckons, shining so bright
Clarion call - comes the Lemurian might
"The Golden Age," in its glorious sight.

Angels gather, standing tall
"Victory to the Light!" they all made their call
Unified in love, peace and harmony for all
The trumpet of victory, breaks the 3D wall.

SOLDIERS OF VIETNAM WAR
By: *Maya The Shaman*

America, I arrived in my teens. A time when Vietnam War persists.
America said they were fighting for their country—'The
Communist Party
they wished to defeat."

In vain were both Vietnamese and Vietcong; people I have to
mention, and American soldiers, too.

American camps blown out by the bombs
American soldiers died by large numbers in their camps.
Left and right Americans shed body parts,
With blood-covered camp floors, walls, and ceilings, too.

My engineer Filipino Father worked for America in Vietnam, an
important role he played.
Keeping power plants running days and nights to keep it safe and
free from harm. Father risked a decade thousands of hours of his
life, in service, away from his family.

Over and over, Father fell on a Vietcong trap
Many snakes waiting where Father dropped
Vietcong snake traps desirable death trap
Many days and nights, snakes pit Father was trapped.

Hunger, thirst, and fear for my Father's life.
Father was Weak and almost lost his life, while

American soldiers rushed to save his life, for an important role,
they all had to partake and complete the task.

Father save American soldiers with his electric generators, a lost
Father, their priority to save him out of the snake pit, too, so he
can serve to generate needed energy, for all his American soldiers in
Vietnam war, too.

Many times, Father had fallen on Vietcong traps
And still survived without a snake bite.
Miracles kept father alive, while the rest were unseen and trapped,
the rest were wounded, and died in war.

American soldiers came back home broken.
Broken limbs, broken bones, broken hearts,
Broken minds and broken Souls
And they knew "War" was not meant for
anyone at all!

POET: Christopher Seiffert

GOLDEN HEART

What's awakening in your golden heart
Is a love whispered in poems
Felt within the soul
A love so grand
So divinely orchestrated
By God and by you
That it lights up every grid of this earth
Creating a pathway through the darkness
Straight to God's heart
You are forever the light
The reminder of the power of love
Blessed and protected from above

BREATHING LIFE
By: *Christopher Seiffert*

We speak of the beauty in this world
As a breathtaking experience
But the love that you share
The ways that you care
Are proof of the truth of your life:
Your heart breathes life into the world
Your heart gives life to the lifeless
Your love reignites the flames
Your love is divine in every way
With every inhale and exhale
You birth the new into reality
You shake the foundation
Of all that is false and untrue
This is the magic of divine love
This is the magic of you

BALANCE
By: *Christopher Seiffert*

Your heart is the anchor
Of Divine Feminine and Divine Masculine
A perfect mix, a perfect blend
The intertwining of earth and cosmic love
Your journey into your heart
Brings a balance to your inner world
Where you dance the intricate and intimate
A meshing of seen and unseen
The sun and the moon
Your heart carries the key
To unlocking your life's mysteries
Where your mission is revealed
Where your pain and trauma is healed
Leading you to your most authentic self

LIFE CHANGING LOVE
By: *Christopher Seiffert*

The deeper you journey into the heart
The more magic and truth is revealed
And what you're finding
And what you've been hiding
Is the most powerful and life changing love
That's ever existed
You see your heart knows the way
Your heart doesn't need protection
It requires freedom and sovereignty
It asks to be felt in its entirety
And to share this love with the world
When your heart is set on fire
Divine love comes alive
And with this love you change the world

HEART ALCHEMY
By: *Christopher Seiffert*

You're a master alchemist of love
In a master class on earth school
Every lesson becomes a beautiful blessing
When you let love and let God
Journey deeper into your heart
Ascend higher into the heavens
Your heart always lighting the way
The darkness is your ally
Your shadow your best friend
Allowing you to integrate fractal pieces
And realize that you are whole
Wholly loved, wholly felt
Holy loved, holy felt
Your story hand written by God
To bring this world to its rightful place
To move through the heart
In a healing space
The container of safety and protection
For God's gift to the collective:
Your heart overflowing with divine love

DIVINE TIMING
By: *Christopher Seiffert*

The heart is never in a hurry
It knows patience
It trusts divine timing
It innerstands the divine plan
And as you connect deeper into your heart
Time itself slows down
You begin to trust the process
You surrender to life
Knowing that all is exactly
As it's meant to be
Trust the pace of your life
Trust the guidance of your heart
Trust in your divine guidance
Trust in your divine protection
Trust in divine love

POET: Patricia Wald-Hopkins

CONVERSATIONS WITH GAIA: FORGIVENESS

What must die within us to be free to create beauty?
Forsake corruption, selfishness, fear and pride
Please forgive us
We know better now
May we begin again
Leading from our hearts
Letting the mind be the servant not the master

Gaia Responds
Child may your body soften and receive my love
You have never ever been forsaken
My love for you is steadfast

I hold you now in a tender embrace of forgiveness
I whisper love into your body through all your senses
 One in ecstatic communion

CONVERSATION WITH GAIA: FEMININE POWER RETURNS

By: *Patricia Wald-Hopkins*

A cavern deep within the earth
The air wet and damp
Smell of minerals, and sound of water
A shadow dances in the low light
A wild woman's face appears
Hidden for thousands of years
Her desire to reclaim her power, freedom and the Voice of her people
The ancient tongue of Gaia
To return to the lands of her ancestors
La Reina Roja
Sangre de Cristo

Gaia Responds
Your feminine power was never lost only misplaced in the darkness of mankind's confusion over where true power resides
True power lives in the heart and the womb of creation
Your return to the world now is symbolic of a greater awakening of true freedom
It is a sign of respect and liberation for all women
Divine Feminine Power is life giving Light upon the Earth being fully returned to all women
It is time to flourish and return to the way of Beauty
Create Heaven on Earth for the children

CONVERSATIONS WITH GAIA: AWAKENING VOICES
By: *Patricia Wald-Hopkins*

My heart beats faster as I gasp for air
One sound, a shriek, a full bodied yell
Freedom is in these sounds of a woman discovering her voice again
The anger in her belly rises as the sacred rage is released with each exhalation and sound
The red hot truth is expressed
And keeps women from ever falling silent again

Gaia Responds
I am in every sound you make my sacred child
Made of me and through me
You are a sacred vessel of my Voice
A unique expression of beauty and grace
Your voice is the water that runs through my rivers and streams into the deep blue sea
Your voice is the gentle whispers of the aspen leaves quaking on the mountain side
Your voice is the verdant green of the jungles and forests
Your voice is the sacred soil upon the desert floor
I hear the birds singing
The coyote howling at the moon
The rain falling upon me
You are a precious reflection of me
Never forget you are meant to be free

CONVERSATIONS WITH GAIA: SEEDS OF NEW EARTH
By: *Patricia Wald-Hopkins*

There is a deep sorrow in my heart
Heavy and wet like the muddy flats after desert rain Heavy and wet and thick with grief
I have seen the disaster coming
If we don't stop this way of life
I have felt it in my bones
The elixir of greed and vanity
The power drug of domination
I hear You softly, yet firmly remind me that humans do not reign supreme
We must learn to plant the seeds of the new earth We are the new earth leaders
The Voices of Gaia
We lead the way
Tending the beauty and honoring all life

Gaia Responds
Yes, slow down
Feel my rhythm under your feet
Feel me breathing through the trees
Taste me in the air
Drink me into your cells
Let deeply nourish you
Let there be a new found joy burst forth from you
Like honey light

CONVERSATIONS WITH GAIA: LIBERATION
By: *Patricia Wald-Hopkins*

Speak the truth boldly at any cost
Reclaim the power that was taken from you as woman
Do not be afraid to be the sovereign Lioness
Freedom, liberation are your birthright
Sacred rage
Liberates your soul

Gaia Responds
Dance with the shadow self
Give her a sacred audience
Give her a sacred stage
Bring forth the blood stories of the women that live within your bones and set them free
Honor the ancient ones that know how to be in communion with earth
Return the patriarchal mental implants of deception
Your sacred rebellion
Liberated woman
Free to speak for equality
Free to be fully seen
Free to fully be a woman of the rose
Healer, seer, oracle, lover, creator
Life force unleashed
Heaven on Earth

CONVERSATIONS WITH GAIA: RISE UP
By: *Patricia Wald-Hopkins*

Blessed be the ones that find the strength within to rise to the occasion to create a new earth
To rise for the feast
The Goddess awaits with resplendent grace
The reward is the unveiling of the golden age
Blessed be the ones unafraid to walk away from greed and vanity
Those that are ready instead to speak the wisdom of the ancient roots of the trees and bod and bones of the ancestors
To usher in the future where sustainability and balance within the whole ecosystem outweighs the need of the individual to be in total dominion of the world

Thanking Mother Gaia for her undying mercy
As we learn and evolve with each breath

Gaia Responds
Gentle children shall rule the earth
And so it is

POET: Deo Palma

MYSTIC LOVE

Your face is shining like a moonlight

Your eyes is twinkling like a million stars

And when you smile

It's colorful rainbow in the sky

I can hear heart beats

Like a blooming flower

In the wilderness tonight

As the birds spread their wings of freedom

Across the blue sky of eternal life

I realized deep inside

That human heart

To God fall in love

DIAMOND IN THE SKY
By: *Deo Palma*

A Beaming light is twilight in sight
where illusion is a real life
Dancing without pain or sorrow in a shadow of the night
Beneath the darkest moon there is a shining light.

Crossing the turbulent ocean of dreams
There is a genuine joy in selfless serving
Touching every hopeful heart to rise
In a place where stars are shining bright.

Where every teardrop is diamond in the sky
Where every breath is a sacrificial fire
Where every heart beat Is precious more than gold
To carry the foreseeable future
Where tyranny vanishes and cruelty is not told.

Rejoice for the time has come where evil are defeated
God's and Goddess celebrates like armored knights
Where humanity becomes the Center of a Universal fight!

CRY NO MORE
By: *Deo Palma*

Today, the nation celebrated your Independence Day
126th Years is not enough to mend the sorrow and pain
Of the heart that knows the tears of sufferings
In darkness, on the allays of loneliness without food and a place called home.

Cry my beloved, when the nation abundant
in beauty and richness
Is denied with the basic necessities of life
Such as food, medicines, clothes, education and shelter!
Cry my Beloved and ask if you are really FREE and independent?

When you can't even decide for your own destiny!
When the poor man's sweat, blood and tears
It is the delicious food of the exploiters and the powerful!
And the nation's flesh becomes a living skeleton.

Cry my Beloved, when you do not even have an Identity
Are you really FREE?

From passive mentally,
inferiority complex and defeatist psychology
And so, you have to make a final STAND!

As the adage goes; FREEDOM is not given...it is taken.
And Beloved, then, Cry NO MORE!

POET: Ebony Shalom xo

UNIVERSAL CONNECTION

In the depths of pain, I found my truth,
A connection deep, a guiding proof.
Through innocence stolen and a shattered heart,
I found a love that would never part.
I questioned the world, I questioned me,
Seeking answers, seeking to see.
And in the silence, the Universe spoke,
Of love that binds, of love that woke.
I didn't seek it, didn't know it was there,
But in my pain, I found it, a love so rare.
A connection to all, a universal embrace,
A reminder of love, in every place.

STARBORN MISSION
By: *Ebony Shalom xo*

From realms beyond, I descend to Earth,
An extra-terrestrial of cosmic birth.
In 3rd density, I find my place,
With a mission to heal, with love's embrace.

Through starlit realms, I journey on,
Bridging worlds where light has shone.
Transmitting, receiving, energies divine,
Guiding humanity to its destined line.

My purpose clear, my path defined,
To raise vibrations, hearts entwined.
A star person's call, to Earth I heed,
With love as my guide, I plant the seed.

TRANSCENDENT PURPOSE
By: *Ebony Shalom xo*

I am the conduit, the vessel of light,
Transcending dimensions, day and night.
Integrating energies, from realms afar,
Illuminating paths, like a shining star.

Between 3rd and 4th, I weave the thread,
Raising consciousness, where love is spread.
Scientific knowledge, poetry's verse,
A symphony of healing, the universe.

My mission statement, clear and bold,
To heal the abuse, as the story's told.
In every interaction, every word I say,
Love's vibration grows, day by day.

A SOUL'S JOURNEY
By: *Ebony Shalom xo*

In the realm where souls reside,
A connection waits, deep inside,
A bridge of light, a sacred door,
To higher vibrations, forevermore.
Through this bond, a dance of grace,
Elevating our hearts, a divine embrace,
It opens our senses, unlocks our sight,
Guiding our journey with celestial light.
When we nourish this soulful tie,
Our spirits soar, reaching beyond the sky,
In harmony, we hear the whispers of truth,
And feel the wisdom, ageless and uncouth.
But should we falter, neglect this bond,
The lower frequencies may respond,
We wander lost, aching and unsure,
Disconnected from what makes us pure.
So let us cherish this connection strong,
Feed our souls, where love belongs,
For in its embrace, we find our way,
Guided by higher vibrations each day.
Together we'll soar, in unity's embrace,
Embracing the light, in every space,
Forevermore, our souls shall be,
A beacon of love, eternally free.

WALK THE TALK IN THE NAME OF LOVE
By: *Ebony Shalom xo*

It is not enough to just believe that love will save our souls.
One must individually face their own fears,
in order for things to unfold.
We cannot expect great changes to take place through passing on
information alone.
We must back these ideas by setting examples,
through our everyday actions; this can be shown.
To not subscribe to the dictated lies,
we must look at ourselves and ask,
"Why am I scared of living my truth?
What prevents me from taking off the mask?"
Whether it's disappointing others,
being rejected or abused, losing work,
loved ones, or owing money...
By recognizing the fears that you've been hiding within,
you will raise yourself and others up—which is key.
Our truth is love; this is our source.
We are co-creators of this reality.
But whilst there are still unmet fears inside us all,
we will continue to cycle with misery.
This message is not a riddle; standing together,
we do inspire!
Just don't be fooled by the fear you hide,
if you are looking to expand and vibrate higher.
We aren't the judgment of others;
we aren't the person we think we are.

We are so much more, and our source is needed now.
Are you ready to help 'raise the bar'?
Stand together and stand-alone, being the example of truth.
Use your knowing to walk the talk, deny the subscribers...
by being the proof.
Love has already won; if you feel these words to be true,
Confront your own fears,
let more light fill your being,
live your truth from love...
BE YOU.

NURTURING DIVINE CONNECTIONS
By: *Ebony Shalom xo*

Through chakras and portals,
we access the team,
In dimensions vast,
where souls shimmer and gleam.
Within the void,
we create and explore,
A divine blueprint,
love's essence we adore.
On our highest timeline,
messages unfold,
From the depths of our soul,
a story untold.
Feeding our physical bodies,
wisdom we gain,
A connection so deep,
it's never in vain.
A relationship born,
between body and soul,
Empowering our being,
making us whole.
Balance restored,
in our natural state,
Nurturing mind,
body, heart, and soul, regenerate.
We recognize our essence,
a soul divine,

Meeting its needs,
a path we align.
Moving forward,
evolving in grace,
Embracing our journey,
finding our place.
So let us cherish the connection we share,
With our spiritual team,
a love beyond compare.
In nurturing our souls,
we find our true worth,
A harmonious dance,
a journey of rebirth.

HEARTFELT UNITY
By: *Ebony Shalom xo*

As these views start putting into action,
The belief of those who know their hearts' satisfaction,
The Earth's noticed beauty and appreciated concern
Will blossom into unity for all those who know,
no earn.
Working together for the future,
placing a heart first for the better,
Overwhelming amounts of hands wanting to give
To renew the life of the patient Earth and belief.
The belief is simple:
Know your instincts and feel.
Trust yourself and your heart.
Love all that you do,
Respecting all on the path.
Criticize nothing; rather,
show you understand
With positive communication,
expressions, and lending hands.
Believe times are tough?
Know to observe life.
Situations that seem threatening—why are they on your path?
Exit the threat and find all that is new.
Listen to your heart; it's your soul speaking with you.

POET: Neil Gaur

THE 5TH WORLD

Meditate and levitate
Waves of frequencies resonate higher
Connected with the provider
Source of cosmic energy
We are going to be
One single entity
Expansion remedied
Oneness must breathe
Exhale and let free
Consciousness to be
Experiences of you and me
Souls of inter-dimensional beings
To feel, hear, and see

This third-dimensional planetary existence...
All time can be seen in one instance
In this realm of linearity
Atoms in anarchy
Quantum polarity
Consciousness duality
The epitome of creation
Ether's imagination
Facing our ego
Acquiring patience
Waiting to let go of our nations
And join the federation of souls
That will take us to the fifth world

THE MISSION
By: *Neil Gaur*

Live life to the fullest
Each day seconds turn in to minutes
Time passes by
Animals and leaves die
Browning by the seasons
Growing and planting seeds again
Is what all men and women are destined to do
In order to continue the life we choose
The sun shines light and we move through the heavens, tunnels and tubes
Worm holes, niches and grooves
Navigating existence so we can enter the womb
In gestation... I AM elation Exhilaration and patience
Creates the balance in this waste land
Of nuclear pollution
My observation of creation
Is that we are all heading in the same destination
Millennia of intergalactic wars
Can't stop the frequency we are in store for
So I spit from the core of my lost fragmented soul
Reclaiming pieces I left in this world
The carrot in front of me, the elusive pearl
I remember
I came here before
Just one emcee.
energetically emanating empathy

Connected to the fire within me
Where I become pure energy
Amnesia in this fallacy
Anesthesia to numb out the insanity
Over stimulation leading to apathy
Speak out against status quo,
accusations of blasphemy
The gravity of third dimensional reality
Causes physical and emotional bankruptcy,
travel the galaxy,
release the agony
Rearrange the anatomy to avoid the catastrophe,
achieve cosmic morality
Embrace the duality is the only analogy
That supersedes all we need
just so that we can let go and breathe

BEING HUMAN
By: *Neil Gaur*

Tears slowly fall down from heaven
Touch five sensory being
Hear this life scream for healing
Locking vibrational frequencies
So I unlock essence with the key
The fragrance of roses
An existence worth living
Asking begging giving
Receiving
Karmically tied obligation
Heart is bleeding
Concrete constructs cave captivity
Created by my soul
Breathing...
Breathe.
I understand
All is forgiven in one breath
Connected to earth
Wind and fire
Passion and desire
Who am I?
Thoughts I do not own
Human impulses shameful being
Still growing, evolving
never accomplished anything
How can one be loved?

Only remembers being pushed and shoved
Third dimensional conditioning
Unconditionally accepting
All of the past has created the NOW
Embrace the self I loathed,
Take the cosmic oath
Pain, struggles and woe Love, abundance
I now know.
What am I.

MOTHER EARTH
By: *Neil Gaur*

This goes out to 1 of the manifestations of source
The north sky reflects light onto my porch, the entire planet is my church
Even when she is scorched, Mother nature will nourish
And replenish the soil, so that mankind can reap the spoils
Creation & Destruction,
the Kali Ma personification manifesting on this plane
In the form of all life
Married to father sky
Our minds remain fertile,
Earth on the back of a turtle
The Nephilim reversal,
and generations of persecution
Nemesis brings retribution,
and Ishtar's contribution
Are the flowers that bloom,
the life that we once knew
She is the one who,
provides unconditional love to you
As we move over her surface,
I dedicate these verses
She is always of service
Time to give back, time to bring it back
The wounded feminine is where we have been at
But also the wounded man, the divine aspect ran
Away from our place a millennia ago,

patriarchy and damaged egos
Took over this world
Now is the moment to bring back the days of old
The divine feminine has been on hold, But never truly left
The energy transcends gender, as we embark on this quest
To remember our nest, before we were born she blessed
You and me... you and me... But who are we?
An illustration of beauty and art
Displayed in the cosmos for all those who pass us
to see and admire
She is the fire, the water, he wind and the birds
All other creatures have heard
Her voice sings land into existence
Providing assistance and gravitational resistance
So we continue to thrive
When we die before our souls return to the sky
We join her become her again,
the truest of friends
With us until the end & rebirth,
She is Mother Earth.

IN THE BEGINNING:
By: *Neil Gaur*

The Void:
In the beginning, there were no words, no concept, no winning
no place, no time, no description, no label and no finishing
until awareness became conscious of itself, no east, no west, no south or north
there never existed a dimension or ascension or physical lessons, only the zero point
there was no Christ to anoint... Singularity energy frequency raised vibrationally
paradoxically into limitation of what the 5 sense can see
No linearity, no anarchy, no galaxies, no nebulae
no jobs, no nature, no materialism, and no political lies
until darkness finally fragmented from the light, using freewill to see through the night
The Darkness:
full of fright...
In my bed,
insecure from the conspiracy that might
take over my mind...control me with a chip inside
scared and full of fear, that is the reason why we are here
to the star system of Arcturus,
I stare and recite my cosmic prayers
self-empowered,
the fabric of victim consciousness I tear
The Light:
The destination has already been chosen,

it's the journey that counts
every day we transcend, no doubt
living in the NOW
a creation of our own subconscious mind,
channel through the heart, remembrance of the divine
take apart my ego and restart my life, in any moment
traveling across the intergalactic ocean,
took the psychedelic potion
now I AM awoken,
to the streets,
we take the spoken
word...
fly high, levitate the god inside,
free like a bird...
Cosmic Oneness Integrating it in my Being,
frequencies inhibit what we are seeing
I shift what I choose to believe

POET: Caroline Roy (Care)

A FRESH START

Today I'm going to be freed
It's time to tend to any weeds
so I may plant the seeds
that aligns with what I need!

LOVING ALL OF YOU
By: *Caroline Roy (Care)*

We desire to be our highest selves
Yet fear embracing all of ourselves.

We have this way of shunning
Our shadows by running.

We make them feel rejected
When in reality, we're mis-directed.

We get taught to shame anything negative
And praise vibes, only when positive.

We're meant to be friends
and have this relationship last till the end.

We need to reframe our views on darkness
So that our biases don't lead us to be heartless.

We can fully love all of who we are
Once we accept our shadow as a co-star.

SHE WANTS TO LIVE!
By: *Caroline Roy (Care)*

While sitting with my shadow, She confessed...
I want to have a seat at the table
I want to live
I want to be seen as able

While sitting with my shadow, She revealed...
I lack the ability to fully rage
I lack the resources to fill my own cup
I lack the key to be freed from this cage

While sitting with my shadow, She expressed...
I need to be healed
I need to be chaotic
I need to be loved

While sitting with my shadow, She declared...
I desire to be free
I desire to be accepted
I desire to be heard without having to agree

While sitting with my shadow, She proclaimed...
I offer you a whole new perspective
I offer you a different set of colours
I offer you a wholesome way to live

And I offer Us, a deeper way of Self-Love!

WITH LOVE
By: *Caroline Roy (Care)*

I see you wanting to play
Yet you're keeping yourself at bay.

I hear you wanting to scream
But worried someone will think you're mean.

Stop letting yourself stay small
For you're worthy of the deepest love of them all!

Always follow the rhythm of your own tune
And let it transport you to the moon.

I witness you and your collection of masks
Instead of letting your authenticity bask.

I cheer for you to shine so bright
As you realize the power of your inner light.

While you fall deeper in love with your being
You'll realize how much less you need to be doing.

So be yourself always and forever
As we rise up with love, all together!

BLOOMING SPRING
By: *Caroline Roy (Care)*

The winds are shifting.
Transitioning from the harshness
of winter's blusters and slumbers
to the clean and cleansing re-birth of spring.

The mating dances are starting up.
As sacral energy reignites
the fires of passion rising up
in the warmth of the sun's rays.

The flowers are emerging for their yearly
center stage moment of full bloom.
Not allowing the weight of melting snow to hold them back
and instead, welcoming the water as fuel for growth.

The birds are flying back in flocks and V's.
The geese honking, the ducks quacking,
the crows cawing, the chickadees chirping,
the robins tweeting, the doves cooing.

Working all together in harmony, as they create
the fragrance, the orchestra,
the colour palette, the texture,
and the flavour of springtime's vibrancy.

ATTUNE
By: *Caroline Roy (Care)*

We don't always invest
into working on feeling our best.
Then, it can turn into being stressed
and we feel it in our chest.

This causes us to divert
sometimes turning to binging on dessert.
Leading us to not wanting to flirt
and inviting us to start to assert.

Instead of turning to complain
more self-compassion to reduce the pain.
Why don't we go dancing in the rain
and let dopamine fill our brain.

It's time to say hello.
To honouring the slow.
So we can come back into full know
and attune with the self-love that we need to flow.

POET: Sandra Basudde

MINE THE HEART

Seek the diamond in the rough
Let go
No attachment
To things that do not last

Enter the portal
And mine the heart
Moments forever
Gems that polish

A mirror reflecting
What IS my heart

TURNING THE PAGE
By: *Sandra Basudde*

Turning the page
What is there of yesterday

Lingering in my mind?

Time passes
As I read to understand
this Wisdom

But holding on
Afraid to let go of what I think to know

Turning the page
The wonder of what has been written

Setting precedent
Yet the future is not etched in stone

Fluid the feeling of joy brings to life animations of creative
exploration

Deep within stirs the Word
AUM
I AM

Turning the page

I be nothing
Now free of definition

Still in this recognition

Eternally seeking in a state of perpetual becoming The Way
Leading
to dimensional adventures
Cosmic in design

LOVE beckons

Lifetime after lifetime

Giving each being that I AM

The universal sound
A means to an end

With new beginnings

Ever to turning the page

POET: Milallan Diipalii Younan

THE SHADOW

The silent shadow is embedded down inside me
Just hiding and living its truth
Neither good nor evil as it should be
But then I harbored all my fears there
Kept my sorrows and pain buried

All my doubts and pessimism locked
I am lost in my own whirlwind of darkness
My breath is strangled as I am facing the end
The air that is free seems not to be
Oh where is the Light?

The other side of my being arise
Then I realize that the same shadow
That can cast darkness can also uphold light
I am that I am
Yes I will shine and glow as my truth

LOVE TRANSCENDED
By: *Milallan Diipalii Younan*

The heart rhymes for the one
With or without a reason breathes for the known and unknown
Ever hidden in the heights and depths yet reveals the rarest light closer

When in silence feelings blossom, In real aloneness buds begin to smile
The cold and the fire battles in deep communion and never surrender to one's power
A time of eternity creeps and awakens

Love has no beginning nor end
What seems to be lost or found, It never was nor will be
It is present as the everlasting time beyond life and death

In a blink the lover and the beloved suddenly disappears and melts
The truth is tasted when only love remains
The fragrance is left for all , Love ascends and descends

When everything is returning as a farewell of hope
Nothing is left but only one is present
It does not move in any path but neither static, The moment is most worshiped

The searcher and the mystery merges not knowing when and where

In the sweetness of the earth, In the holiness of the heavens
Deeply as LOVE TRANSCENDS

GHOST RIDER
By: *Milallan Diipalii Younan*

The elements of life and death quiver in every breath
Struggling to survive in the eyes of the tempest
Every stone drips blood and sucks the verve, who can feel what is real?

The unknown always remains a legend unfolding a new chronicle every century
Leaving a mystery that drives the spirit to be free and be tested either to fail or survive
Who can truly live?

Since the beginning of consciousness the eyes try to enter every window and door
For eternity is beyond limits but every step just brings closer to the end
Who can pass?

The time has come when words just become water so light and liberated
Waiting to be dissolved in its power and merge with the wind
Who can truly hold?

Then the heart is the only weapon: The nucleus of the being
But those who believe lives in a dream, Everyone is asleep yet denies

Who can be awakened?

Illusions bestow a gravity to valiant to resist for it is the way to see matters that exist
But what is authentic is a ghost that rides in every soul so silent and deep
Who can truly see?

LIFE'S MOMENT
By: *Milallan Diipalii Younan*

A moment is always precious
Memories will always be treasured
And years will be remembered
In every timeline, who and what is forever there?

Life unfolds a million changes
Tides may reverse and distort feelings on one side
On the other, mysteries may uplift the spirit
To keep the soul alive
Do you feel something and one thing unchanged?

The heart may keep on searching
As the golden star is hidden
The only diamond is lost and taken
Will you ever try to hold on and remain?

When I see your eyes smile
And hear your silence speaks
Even in a whisper, the song enters
It is God's love that is present

THE SILENCE
By: *Milallan Diipalii Younan*

The silence of the river
Flows in the freedom
Carried by the wind and merges in Your love

The music of my cry
Melts the sun in your eyes
It brings joy to my heart and unites in Your mind

All my life I have been searching
But I need to go nowhere
You are deep within my soul
And I can't exist without you

The sweet scent of my dreams
Reveals the magic of my quest
I tried to know its meaning
I could not understand

Yet I feel complete
And forever lost in Your mystery
It is a question without an answer
Only to feel that you are there
How could I ask for more

INNER VISION
By: *Milallan Diipalii Younan*

At times the eyes gaze
Through the unknown, vast and endless
The vision that could only be guided
By the knowledge of the stars
As dreams spirally soar and dive

Miracles and promises may be near
As the moon is so close to see
Yet too far to grasp
The mind in chaos sparks
The heart in revolution marches

Everyday the journey differs
But the traveler is never altered
Expressing changes in gray and hue
Moments slip to memories
Life evolves as well as it descends

ONE TRUTH
By: *Milallan Diipalii Younan*

The matter reaches places
Mind travels beyond matters
And all these destinations
Lead to one sanctuary
An abode of eternity

There may be thousands of beliefs
Each shining a peculiar color
To complete the earthly home
But to what question one yields
There is only the truth

That is, you are, I am
In simplicity existence blossom
In space evolution transcends
No words are being said nor manifested
In nothingness there is only you and you

MYSTIC TRAVELER'S NEW BEGINNING
By: *Milallan Diipalii Younan*

You can only feel true bliss
When you were once drown in burning fire
You can only see the brightest light
When you were once imprisoned in the darkest asylum
You can only be totally free
When you were once chained by the heaviest metal
And you can only feel true love
When you were once devoured by scorching ire

The ice will not freeze you
The sky will not drop you
The water will not drown you
The fire will not burn you
The earth will not devour you
All these elements are inside you
That form the source of life in the universe

Ultimately, death will not cease
But will liberate and free you
To enter and realize the known and unknown
Just become and be your truth

BELIEVE YOU
By: *Milallan Diipalii Younan*

Believe who you are
Even your eyes may be veiled with injustice
Your mind may be tainted with lies
But your truth is liberating

You desire for wealth and gain
Fame and power to be at your fingertips
It is so triggering and heartbreaking
Like the moon to see but not to hold

Is there a key to unlock the secret
If so, where to find and what it is
Look into your heart simply
The answer is as pure as the lamb

Yet the mind yearns for gold
The material powers unfold
The inner voice tells love, Is it enough there
and stop?

What if two dimensions could unite
Money and love to no question and doubt
A light that cuts and splits beyond the duality of the mundane
The tangible and intangible churn into one embodiment

MORNING GRACE
By: *Milallan Diipalii Younan*

In the early morning
The sweet beginning
I wake up by your grace
Only Your name I call and sing

You are the morning grace
You are the infinite source
You are the colors of the rainbow
You are the rhythm of my life

As the sunshine smiles in my heart
Or the rain's music falls in my eyes
I will and forever wake up by Your grace
Only Your name I call and sing

As I welcome the moonlight
I hope to greet tomorrow
By Your everlasting grace
Only Your name I call and sing

FOR ETERNITY
By: *Milallan Diipalii Younan*

Life is always filled with streaming desires
That at times may cloud the essence of existence
Or could lift the consciousness in blooming spirit
Whatever the journey leads to
There is one thing unchanged

The heart dances in a tapestry of emotions
The mind is stormed by doubts, fears and propensities
Will a portal open to a beginning or end
The answer may rest in a question
To be lived and experienced for eternity

POET: Radhaa Nilia

ROYALTY

In Egypt's time of wealth and might,
I lived a life of royal sight.
A woman in a world of men,
I fought to prove my worth again and again.
Amidst the battles and the wars,
I stood my ground on Egypt's shores.
A warrior fierce, a leader bold,
I fought for my people, strong and old.
But even in the midst of glory,
I knew the dangers of my story.
For those who wished to see me fall,
We're always waiting for their call.
And in the end, I met my fate,

A victim of their cruel, twisted hate.
The fall was hard, the pain was deep,
But still, my spirit refused to sleep.
For though my body may be gone,
My spirit lingers, carries on.
And even now, so many years ahead,
I still feel the echoes of the words they said.
The hatred still can cut so deep,
But still, I rise, I do not weep.
For in the end, I know it's true,
My strength and spirit carried through.
So if you too have felt the pain,
Of a past life where you were slain,
Take heart, my friend, and rise again,
For in the end, you will ascend.

A FEILD OF DREAMS
By: *Radhaa Nilia*

In the field of dreams, under skies so wide,
Where love blooms like wildflowers, side by side.
You in a cowboy hat, rugged and true,
Me in cowgirl boots, ready for our debut.

In dreams, we embrace, though yet to meet,
A life together, vibrant and sweet.
A big, beautiful family we envision,
Our home alive with love's precision.

On a hill with acres, our haven stands tall,
Welcoming loved ones, one and all.
Space to breathe, where hearts entwine,
An art and dance studio, where dreams align.

Here we dance beneath the stars,
To the melody of love, with no bars.
In your embrace, I find my rest,
A sanctuary, where we're truly blessed.

I always dreamed of my own family,
And now with you, it's a reality.
In this haven, our love will bloom,
A testament to dreams that loom.

We celebrate our love, a bond unseen,

A world shared with you, our secret, serene.
In a journey forged from broken pasts,
We found strength in love that lasts.

For I waited, in the quiet of night,
For a soul like yours, my heart's delight.
Proposed to, but never said yes,
For marriage, to me, means nothing less.

It's a union divine, where souls align,
In the past, your heart was mine.
Now found in this life, our paths converge,
In a dance of love, a sacred urge.

I waited for you, my beloved, it's true,
In fields of dreams, where vows are due.
Though we haven't met, my love's so true,
For better or worse, I stand by you.

Past hurts forgotten, our love, a bliss,
A blessing we share, a gentle kiss.
In your arms, I've found my peace,
In your love, all pain is released.

So here's to us, to love's embrace,
To a future bright, a sacred space.
In this poem, our hearts entwine,
In this love, forever, you are mine.

THE GALACTIC ROSE
By: Radhaa Nilia

In the vast expanse of space so wide,
Blooms a rose with cosmic pride.
Petals shimmer, stars entwined,
In the darkness, it brightly shines.

Born from nebulae afar,
Fed by light of ancient stars.
Each petal, a story told,
Of galaxies, bright and bold.

Stems stretch out in zero-g,
Rooted in infinity.
Thorns that guard, bright as suns,
Spark like light from ancient runs.

In the Milky Way, it grows,
A miracle, this galactic rose.
Planets turn, comets dance,
All in the rose's cosmic trance.

Its fragrance, a celestial breeze,
Whispers through the endless seas.
Dreams of universes start,
Held within its fiery heart.

Reflecting hues of nebula blue,

Cosmic winds that softly blew.
A flower of eternal grace,
A symbol in the vast embrace.

In space's silent, endless night,
The galactic rose holds tight.
An emblem of the beauty vast,
In the universe, it's unsurpassed.

THE ANCIENT TREE
By: *Radhaa Nilia*

In a forest, calm and old,
Stands a tree with stories told.
Roots run deep, unseen below,
Branches high, where soft winds blow.

Leaves like whispers in the night,
Catch the moon's soft, gentle light.
Bark is rugged, worn with age,
Marking time like a sage.

Through the years, seasons turn,
Lessons hide in every fern.
Spring brings blossoms, fresh and bright,
Summer days, warm with light.

Autumn leaves in colors bold,
Winter's chill, ice and cold.
Yet the tree stands firm and tall,
Witness to the rise and fall.

Generations come and pass,
Moments fleeting, like blades of grass.
Yet this tree, ancient and wise,
Watches under shifting skies.

Oh, if it could tell its tale,

We'd hear of storms and gentle hail,
Of whispers shared and secrets kept,
Of the many tears it's wept.

But in silence, it will stay,
Rooted firm, come what may.
A sentinel, a guardian, free,
An ancient, steadfast, knowing tree.

ALMOST SISTERS
By: *Radhaa Nilia*

Oh, I remember you, when we were small,
Visiting you in foster care, not saying much at all.
You had beautiful, curly black hair, I stayed quiet
    too, but my love was there.
Sadness struck when they took you away,
Mom tried to adopt you, but the system said, "No
    way."
They sent you to a preacher and his wife, A house
    full of kids, but secrets and strife.
Bad things happened there in the night, I felt it in
    my dreams, waking with fright.
I wanted to save you, just a kid too, In East Palo
    Alto, not much I could do.
Letters I sent, month after month, wishing you
    were near,
Pictures of my life, hoping you'd hear.
Silence stretched on, all those lonely years,
A heartbroken girl from a place of tears.
Trauma you felt, seeping so deep, Shaping who
    you were, even in sleep.
When we met again, teens and twenty, I thought
    we were family, love was plenty.
But behind my back, you caused me pain,
    Leeching on me, driving me insane.
Years of betrayal, twenty long years, Love turned
    to sorrow, dreams turned to tears.

Guilt washed over when you told your tale, My
    dreams were true, I felt I'd failed.
I'm sorry for your pain, it hit so hard, Opening my
    heart left me scarred.
You were my sister, I wanted nothing more,
But your actions hurt me, left me my heart tore
How I wonder what we could have been,
If trust and love had always been our kin.
If you loved me with purity just as I loved you.

IN MY RISE
By: *Radhaa Nilia*

In the ashes of a thousand falls,
I've learned the art of standing tall.
Each shattered piece, a lesson learned,
In every crack, new strength was discerned.
From the ruins of my former self,
I gather courage, wisdom, and wealth.
A thousand ways I've been undone,
Yet through each trial, a new me spun.
I've tasted pain in myriad forms,
But from its depths, resilience forms.
With every blow, I rise again,
A testament to strength within.
For in destruction's fiery blaze,
I find the seeds of brighter days.
A thousand ways to rebuild anew,
Each scar a mark of what I've been through.
So let the storms and tempests roar,
I'll rebuild stronger than before.
In every fracture, every crack,
I forge my path and never look back.
The Goddess has my back, so sworn,
I rise from the ashes, reborn.
In the face of trials, I stand and fight,
Blooming brightly in the darkest night.
From the ashes, watch me ascend,

A thousand ways, no less, my friend.
With hope and love as guiding light,
I soar beyond each past regret,
In every fall, a chance to climb,
Creating beauty one more time.

POET: Diya Marie Miller

HEALING IS FOREVER

Touch me soon
Touch me now
Touch me there
Touch me here
Touch me forever
What a fool I was
Touch is temporary
Love me soon
Love me now
Love me there
Love me here
Love me forever
What a fool I was

Love is temporary
Forgive me soon
Forgive me now
Forgive me there
Forgive me here
Forgive me forever
What a fool I was
Forgiveness is temporary
Forgiveness, Love & Touch are interchangeable
Heal me soon
Heal me now.
Heal me there
Heal me here
Heal me forever
I am no fool.
HEALING IS FOREVER

UNLEARNING
By: *Diya Marie Miller*

My exit sealed the portal
Leaving me wet, cold, and trembling

As I slid through the new threshold
Light streamed from my awakening consciousness toward the void
where comforting darkness dwelled

Darkness had been my refuge

Will this journey,
fraud with trials and tribulations
Be safe beyond the womb?
Tuesdays unnamed child
Born in turmoil
Begins a story yet to unfold and unlearn.

POET: JOAN OF ANGELS

THE MOTHER IN ME

The mother in me, the mother I am,
Became a motherless daughter, long ago.
Where did the daughter go?
And...how did I become a mother of a daughter?

So many ways to mother:
Mother your daughter, your mother, your pets, your friends, your trees.
But do not forget to mother the heart of the mother.
Go deep inside the womb where we began.

Who mothered the very first mother?
If we trace back time, she is the original mother,

Created like Eve, the first of the ancestral line.

As I sit in the garden with my children,
What is one mother, divided between two children?
And the grandmothers, oh the grandmothers,
Creating memories, juicy and sweet.

A granddaughter, the child of a mother, birthed from a mother
The mother is the seed, the creator of all.
Who was the first seed, egg, spark?
More to ponder in the garden,
A mother, a daughter, a lineage of light.

DAUGHTER OF THE NILE: A TRANSFORMATION UNVEILED
By: *Joan of Angels*

In dreams, my mother's voice did softly call,
A vision bathed in light, a mystic thrall,
"Child of Cleopatra, you shall be,
A beacon of beauty, grace for all to see."
From a shy and awkward duckling, I did rise,
To shine as radiant stars in boundless skies,
A journey from darkness to a light so bright,
A transformation, awakened by the night.
In memories, I danced as Hathor's grace,
A goddess of beauty, in every face,
Joy, dancing, and delight, I did bestow,
In every heart, my presence made them glow.
And with Isis, goddess of magic's art,
I wove a tapestry, a work of heart,
Mystery and wonder, in every spell,
In the realm of enchantment, I did dwell.
With Hathor's spirit, Cleopatra's bloodline too,
I bear the legacy of queens, both old and new,
To bring healing and balance to the world's embrace,
Resonating beauty, love, and boundless grace.
A star being born from Nile's ancient stream,
In every soul, I light a sacred gleam,
For I am the daughter of Cleopatra here to share,
The gifts of love, beauty, and magic rare.

POET: Cristal Ortiz

YEMANA

A great and powerful mother
is my mother.
She is able to guide, nurture
and protect like no other.
A spiritual mother, celestial
and nautical mother;
To me, and many others.

If ever there has been a strife in my life
she is the one to calm the seas
and carry me through
with her whimsical breeze.

Whenever I have felt somber,
or have life decisions
that require a good ponder...
I never falter to sit by the water,
to remember I am her daughter.

Some may say she is a cryptid entity;
I say that's because they lack
the spiritual sensory to invite in
such fluid complexity
As her serenity is powerful enough
to help guide anyone's destiny.

To me, she is vivid,
with a love that flows like a warm liquid,
Saturating me from head to toe,
allowing me to both grow and glow;
A love powerful enough to ward off all foes.

The color blue was chosen by her
to remain in my veins;
As a notion that I was chosen to be woven
into the eternal ocean she reigns,

An omen of her maternal love
that can be felt
on both the external and internal planes.
Did I forget to mention,
her divine number seven is a sign from heaven
That helps strengthen one's intuition,
As a symbol to know that things dreamt
shall come to fruition?

She is a pristine queen dressed in bright white
that can be seen in the darkest of nights.
She has the tenacity to diminish any plight
humanity may encounter,
If only they hold the capacity to ask her
without falter.

Yemaya is her name.

A name that holds much fame
not only in this world,
but in all domains.

POET: WENDY RAMIREZ

MOTHER'S WILL: A TAPESTRY UNBOUND

At twenty, a mother,
with dreams in her eye,
A babe in her arms,
she watched hope take flight.
Through trials she danced,
with resilience untold
Motherhood's rhythm,
her story unfolds.

Fifty's silvered touch,
a chapter unfurled,
Accounting's pursuit,
a dream in the world.
No mountain too high,
no fear could impede,
Determination's fire,
a passionate creed.

Love's melody shifted,
a family embraced,
Two spirits entwined,
a future embraced.
Education's contract,
a pact to ignite,
Daughter's artistry,
son taking a flight.

Husband, a scholar,
with wisdom to share,
Firstborn, a chef,
with culinary flair.
A tapestry woven,
with love as its thread,
Unbound by age,
their triumphs are spread.

POET: LISA LITTLETON SAMSON

INITIATION

I lost the last embryo, but never my light
Like the harshest Initiation, I bled for 33 nights
In the pit of the well I meet Grandmother and understand it was
Destiny
Loss on loss through generations passed down to me

Through blurred vision river tears now I can see, the Alchemy
comes from me
I reach out my hand through the bloody sea.. the circle of
Priestesses have been waiting

I thought I knew Darkness before, but now she becomes me

But there's one ember deep inside and Priestess me will never let
it die
Not this time, not with this Angel Baby by my side

This Lioness rises, she joins her pride
She fans the ember, she's on the mend
Two turns of the moon and she's with child again

Here it comes, Darkness swallows up my head
The fear demons taunt me I will lose it again
For a moment the worries imprison the shell shocked me within

But Goddess has spoken, and She was an Earth Mother, too
Trust the nightmare is transmuted, now accept the waking dream
come true
Embers turn to flames burning out the darkness
I thank the black that helped me remember the strength I've had
forever

She's resilient, She's Empress, She's Mother again

WAKING DREAM
By: *Lisa Littleton Samson*

I dance my Baby to the rhythm to sleep
Bow to the dark moon, the last cycle complete
Who I was is no longer me, tears stream

I know soon I'll have to share you with the world
So I cherish these tired moments
Our middle of the night dances together won't last forever
It's tender and it's fleeting
Your heavy eyes close now

With you in my arms, all times freeze
When you latch on to me, in sync we breathe, now I know true peace
We're exactly where we're supposed to be

You're my waking dream come true
Only God Herself could have created you
My night sky turned baby blue, my girl you're a waking dream come true

You get all of me, Honey Bear
And when I've given you my all, still I dig deep
Ancient Mother strength courses through my being
I evolve into a Higher Me as I connect to every womb in the tree

I dance you to the rhythm to sleep
I am every Mother and she is me, and you will always be my Baby

RENEWAL
By: *Lisa Littleton Samson*

We've had it all, and we've been of simple needs
It always comes back to you & me, and we made a family

Our love is a seed
Our child is the fruit
Aeris
We are on her tree forever branches wrapped together
Etched in eternity three hearts beat as One

I'm the Moon, you're the Sun
Aeris is An Earth Full of Flowers

I vow to always water our rainbows and greens, to be patient and sweet
To not let the temporary harshness of life overtake the real me
To learn and grow, stay balanced and even
And always enjoy the Garden of Eden, the Earth Full of Flowers

I vow to stay in my power, to bring out the best in me & you
To support the ways you uniquely move through life, forever stand at your side a proud Wife
I'm your ride or die, your Bonnie to Clyde
You're a magic man and I'm down with every plan

I vow to do everything to nurture our tree, I devote myself to the betterment of our family

I devote myself to you, my Husband, our life is a waking dream
come true
Let's enjoy every day, we dance through everything that comes
our way
We're to the Moon, we're boundless, we're bountiful... I love you

POET: Dennis Freese

THE FEAST
By: Dennis Freese

Last night, we ate a cauliflower,
carrots and collards from the garden,
and I picked kale for the chickens,
so that we could all share in this,
the second feast of Spring.

The first, oh, that was for the eyes..
beginning with the brave crocuses
of yellow and purple that lift
their heads above the snow
and alert the daffodils
of their impending call time to

the stage.

From there, the feast of color unfolds with dwarf iris, grape hyacinth and tulips, followed by lilacs of purple and white, whose visual beauty is exceeded only by their fragrance, so utterly sweet, that for long moments was suspended, and the long winter, just a disappearing Ice flow off the continental shelf.

LEAP
By: *Dennis Freese*

It's said that one cannot step
into the same river twice,
but can we even step into the
the same river once?

All is in flux; an apparition
that mind cannot hold,
a moveable feast of
fathomless feats,
Jimi's hassle castle
made of sand.

And yet, everything we seem
to know and love appears
in this space and time
motion machine.

Wow! What a set-up for suffering!
At the end of the daze, though,
what was the distance from the
head to the Heart?

Ten thousand lifetimes in a fraction
of a second!

VIVID
By: *Dennis Freese*

I rarely remember dreams,
but last night was different:
A friend came to me,
and asked if I'd heard
the news about the
man in prison who
had once wounded
our family so deeply?
He has cancer,
and is suffering
terribly as it spreads.
Was this a moment
to say or even think
that karma had come
to collect accounts due?
In the end, the only sin
is ignorance, and how
could ignorance be a
sin?
I felt sadness.

THE GREATEST SURPRISE
By: *Dennis Freese*

I know a man of formless form
as clear as sky is blue.
So simple in his wizened ways
that children see it, too.
And yet, with roots more deeply set,
than even time can reach,
He says more in a silent glance,
than any book can teach.
I know this sounds like that old tale
we learned in Sunday Mass,
Except the one I speak of,
isn't drawn up from the past.
Here's the kicker. Are you ready?
Strip away a layer or two...
Direct into the core of the Heart:
Welcome Home..
T'was ever you!

THE CHILDREN SHALL LEAD
By: *Dennis Freese*

Stopping to internalize forgiveness
for my transgressions,
and those who have trespassed against me,
I wondered how to shape that clay of emotion
into a perfect vessel, fire it in the kiln
of my heart, fill it with the nectar of every flower
in my garden, and offer it to the great
mystery of being.

Staying with that question, I enter my FB page
(in route to our poetry portal), and happen to view
the following report, just posted by my daughter.

*"My new laptop was lost/stolen when I arrived in NYC 3 weeks ago.
It's tough not having a computer! I was hoping someone would do
the right thing and return it, but then I am extremely GRATEFUL
to have a replacement.
I didn't want to get a new one until I was sure it would not be
returned.
It's always a weird feeling when someone has something so personal,
but may they be BLESSED! They may need it more than I do."*

The great mystery readily and instantly offered the
pathway to resolving what I had sought:
"Just ask your daughter how this is done!"
I bow in humility and gratitude.

RATTLER
By: *Dennis Freese*

The journey of a thousand meters, nearly ended in a single step. Whatever took over in that instant, it was not a contemplative mind.

Svāhā
By: *Dennis Freese*

Having...
Tasted every flavor
of Haagen Dazs,
Savored the sweetest kisses
of my beloved,
Shared the intimate language
of music, with friends who
often had no common
spoken tongue,
Beheld stunningly beautiful
earthly sites and smells,
Witnessed the births of three children,
Watched them each flower into
amazing, caring adults,
Experienced all of this
and now...

Looking at an older man's face
in my morning mirror,
What remains of purpose?
Only this:
To emerge from this chrysalis
of dreams, and sail
on butterfly wings,
beyond the boundaries
of time,

or as a salt doll,
diving into the Ocean,
seeking to measure
its' depth and singing:
gate gate pāragate
pārasaṃgate bodhi
svāhā

ON THE CLOSING OF OUR POETRY GROUP
By: *Dennis Freese*

A virtual family reunion
with friends I'd never met,
and never knew existed
until my feet were finally wet.
How strange the times we live in,
we tap dance on our keys,
then push the magic button,
our spirits to appease,
And instantly, the depth of hearts
are measured on a page,
our humor, hopes, and Don Quixotes,
our wonder and our rage.
I'm not the sentimental type,
I reassure myself,
so get a grip, man up,
and leave emotion
on the shelf!
But this is not a forum
to hide in thin disguise,
You've shared with me
so openly, there's
welling up of eyes.
The veil has slowly lifted,
cynicism out the door,
and though I'll only say this once
'I love you to the core!'

- 5:75 -
By: *Dennis Freese*

Awake and arise
Awake from the arising
Dreaming, I'm awake!

POET: Alanna Starr Shimel

IF YOU COME TO ME

If you come to me, my heart is open,
Ready for love, ripe and unbroken.
I'll embrace you with warmth from within,
Choosing to love, again and again.
Prayers for strength, to bear the load,
Without losing self on life's winding road.
If my cup's not full, I cannot give,
But overflowing, happily we live.
Witnessing sorrow, longing to mend,
Offering solace, a soul to tend.
In surrender, suffering finds its place,
Hope whispers softly, in time's pace.
Life's clarity, a precious gift,

Knowing all things, the Great Spirit lifts.
In a sacred way, we return to One,
Miracles rise with frequencies spun.
Liberation in the will to choose,
A divine plan, we cannot lose.
When worlds collide or we ache inside,
Hidden Wisdom is there to guide.
If you come to me, my heart's a book,
In its pages, lessons that it took.
In honor of our resurrection,
I see you, I love you, no condition.
In Lak'ech Ala K'in, unity clear,
Without each other, no reflection here.

THE SCARS OF MY MOTHER
By: *Alanna Starr Shimel*

Mama's scars etched in my DNA,
Lessons of ancestors deep.
Did I choose this life, or was I sent for a mission?
The pain, the purpose, the questions unanswered.
Healing, the wheel of life spins, endless.
From darkness, Wisdom blooms, guiding us home to our Divine Self.
Transmuting ancient wounds, we journey back to love, forgiveness, and reconciliation.
We are everything and nothing, mind, body, spirit intertwined.
Exploring within, discovering our truth, our purpose.
We are the dreams of our Mother's inner child, destined to play life's game.
Holy Mother Divine, within and without, guides us in service and celebration of life.
Open the Gates of Heaven, for Earth is no longer a prison.
We are sovereign, saviors of the realm.
Mother's wounds now healed, peace prevails as intended.
Light codes awaken within, no turning back.
Let Heaven manifest, laying Mother's scars to rest.

SPARKS OF HER

By: *Alanna Starr Shimel*

Each one, a piece of Her, a memory, a gospel, a story to tell.
How She soared on high, then fell.
From girl to woman,
From tiara to crown,
A Goddess in bloom.
Life-giving portals, adorned with love.
Each a spark of Her, embellishing the material.
Though many come to take, She knows no bounds.
Always around, in and out, between worlds.
Her heart sings when we pray.
Her endless love emerges from within,
Awaiting all Her sparks, to hear Her call,
The question lingers heavily, will they be recovered?
The Lover, the Fool, the Priestess, the Magician,
The Emperor and Empress, Kundalini arisen.
Once hidden in darkness, now come to light,
Forgiving misfortunes, balancing scales.
She, as One with the Father, on a sacred mission,
Realizing Her vision, our Makers revision.

POET: Hjalti Kristinsson

JOURNEY OF LIFE

felt the opening, the opening into a new abyss of dreaming,
searching, flowing
being in-side nothingness, yet everything
going through, being through, wanting through
not done, not done, more to be done
no urge, but wish, steadfast, firmfast, being fast
being fist, flowing fist, palms open, opening, inviting
igniting, welcome, seeing welcome, being welcome
seeing threshold, welcoming courage, igniting courage
welcoming strength, taking the step, taking the step being the
step, going through, being there, being here
I am here, I am here

Smileingness, beingness, happiness, calmness
hereness
I am here
I am home

WITH LOVE
By: *Hjalti Kristinsson*

travel through waters of space
swim, flow, flow, be
flow, flow, feel line through, direct through
be through, flow through,
see the point, be the point, being the point
feel the shake, the handshake, the connection
both sides, circle sides, multi sides, all sides
focus point, pivot point, pressure point,
flow point, be point, touch, touch, TOUCH
feel, explode, explode and expand
dimensiate, perpetuate, annunciate, opengate
key is you, key is in you, key is with you, key is you the doors are
here, for you to open, choose next door explore with love, be with
love, be love, be you, Be I

CONNECT
By: *Hjalti Kristinsson*

comunicate - co-mun-i-cate
open - flow - speak - calm
calm - speak - flow - be - open
glow - heart - glow - shine
feel shine land and meet on surface of receptance
feel receptance, receive, shine
like flower receives, opens to sun's rays
you receive heart glow's shining
embrace love, nurturing, gifts within
feel all receiving, all embracing, all glowing
connect all, within, connect all, all is one, alisone
you are me, I am you, feel the flow, feel the dis-flow
combine with love, healing love, flow combined
flow in love, all in love, all is love, all is one, alisone
i am - I am

POET: Leah Sonaria

HIEROS GAMOS

Your eyes are oceanic portals
Summoning Horus and Ra
Merging god and mortal
And awakening the Ka

Deep wells of remembrance
Opening doorways of truth
Becoming teachers of temperance
And sustainers of youth

Guided by Mother's dark light
My rose finds its way to you
Our souls yearning to unite

In a garden made for two

Across galaxies and lifetimes
Sonic threads weave cosmic cloaks
To reactivate Gaia's leylines
And adorn the Goddess she invokes

Isis takes me under her wing
To reveal our star path of destiny
A Queen ennobled to her King
Fused in ecstatic alchemy

Shekinah the Christed dove
Liberates mysteries etched in stone
To resurrect the highest forms of love
And reclaim royal blood and bone

POET: Emmanuel Itier

LIKE AN ETERNAL

Late at night,
When the storm passed by,
And the peace dove flies high,
I see the ghost of you,
Teasing my shivers,
Calming down the shadow of my fevers.

Forever I'll wait,
Dreaming ever after,
For the moment to never end,
When I reach for your hand,
Beyond the gates of heaven,
Like an eternal, blasting Eden.

In the morning's early light,
With only your perfume's scent in sight,
And my faith tested and bent,
I see the ghost of you,
Wedding my shadow,
Calming down the shreds of my sorrow.

Life with you is eternal,
Not a black hole abyss,
Like your deep velvet French kiss,
You and I, like an eternal bliss.
Glory.

ECHOES OF YOUR PRESENCE
By: *Emmanuel Itier*

Under the rain, I've waited,
For the moment it all dissipates,
To feel the warmth of home,
Let my death wash away the pain.

Dreaming beneath Mars' glow,
For the moment it all unfolds,
To banish every fear,
Let my life guide you past the stars.

Like a desperate absence,
A ghost of a romance, sealing fate,
In a slow vertigo, drifting out of state,
Meaning in this nonsense,
An eternal cosmic dance.

Under the sheets, I've lingered,
For the moment solitude fades,
To erase the ache of loneliness,
Let my death vanish in the streets.

Dreaming within your embrace,
For the moment our worlds align,
For the feeling of belonging,
Let my life lead you into dreams.

Like a desperate absence,
An end-of-century chance,
Memories of burning desires,
In a slow vertigo, our love untamed.

Like a shadow of incense,
An eternal cosmic trance.

OCEAN'S REVERIE
By: *Emmanuel Itier*

Let the ocean take me down,
Fill my body with purest air,
Rushing under my skin,
Keeping alive my dream longer.

Wash my brain with a perfect wave,
Letting me forget the pain,
Spread honey down your curves,
Glory to you, my beautiful.

Glory to me, your soul,
And to the mysteries above,
Shaping our destinies.

Let the ocean take me backstage,
Move my spirit with the guitar's riff,
Drown away the myth,
Keeping alive the reality of my rage.

Glory to you, my promised land,
Glory to me, your wonder friend,
And to the insanities below,
That shape our destinies.

Let the ocean turn me to stone,
Build you a throne with my blood,

Be your kingdom,
May your wishes come home.

Glory to you, my beautiful,
Glory to me, your soul,
And to the mysteries above,
Shaping our destinies.

Glory to your glorious day,
Glory to my eternal journey.

POET: Chrystina Box

HOUSE WARMING

Welcome to my home,
Where you will find you are not alone.
Have a seat right here
If you look to the left
You will see a young girl
Dancing and singing joyfully,
Free, in the kitchen
As she lets the music flow through her.
Her dances are endless
She embodies inspiration
Her dances– her voice–
Are for her (not for you)
If you ask her why she won't perform outside,

She'll tell you:
"I don't need the attention."

Let's go to the living room,
Formerly a place of chaos
Where you never knew what words would hurt you
But the woman sitting on the couch, cuddled up
With a warm blanket and a book
Knows how to rest, how to create peace
as she appreciates the quiet.

And now the hallway (a secret pathway)
Leading to common spaces of connection
Away from the bedroom of isolation

In the room at the end of hall
You will see an empty bed;
It is both my friend and my enemy.
Here, I often found myself lost in my thoughts
while I was consumed by my past.
The bed was not always empty:
Once upon a time, there was a couple who seemed happy.
Later on, it became a place of deprivation.
He was a lie, even as I lay with him.
Now, without him, the bed feels fuller, peaceful,
but it is still missing someone.

It was a long way back,
The hallway dark,
For me to see
I was enough for myself.

Come back, please; let's sit back down.
If you feel like waiting for a while,
You will meet, coming through the door,
Many who will love me for myself
And who knows?
You might be one of them.

POET: Selma Harwell

THE GODDESS EXPRESS

Goddess arise from within The spirit of you that has always been And ever shalt be

Be the goddess you are For you've come so far Having risen the bar In front of you

Give in To yourself Step up! Step in! To the self That is ever you

Shining from the inside out Shine brightly light fairy, Lightly

Inwardly blessed Gracefully pressed Truly expressed!

You of the skies That never dies Sometimes hidden In disguise

Goddess arise from within

The spirit of you that has always been And ever shalt be...

Delightful

Go through the setbacks
Meant for query
Then listen and
You are less the worry

The wings of prayer
You get to borrow
Each time you gratefully
Relinquish sorrow

Listen and flee,
Not away -but near glee

Free your soul and just be...

Goddess arise from within
The spirit of you that has always been And ever shall be!

WOMEN PROMOTING WOMEN
By: *Selma Harwell*

Dedicated to Princess Diane and Mother Teresa
September 20, 1997

Women loving, Women Caring
Women loving, Women Sharing

Women usurped by possessive violence
Now burning with life, no longer silent

Eager to serve, promoting others
Women as fathers, Women as mothers
Devoting their vanity for the aid of humanity
From 4 Directions around the globe

Transformations spilling with hope
Balancing discordance assisted by man
Gently persuading however we can
Voluptuous Curves, Sensuous Ways
creating futures each and every day

With what we were given to be driven

Women in Art, Theater, Dance
Beauty abounds to give us a chance
Expressing our voices with grace and agility
Now for the world of All-Possibility

Women as Partners saving our ethics
Focusing love, breeding acceptance.
Women as Healers Endless Wisdom
Solutions of the ages- take time to listen

Women empowered Women with Soul
Determined Purposeful Centered Whole

OVERWHELMING JOY
By: *Selma Harwell*

Overjoyed in gratitude of living well in good health

Standing for enjoyment of every moment

No small task is no biggy either

Take that moment to pause and breathe

In the pause you access pause-ativity and become

"Pause"- ative ahhh!

Breathe in silence.

Breathe-in silence

Breathing silently

Calming, centering, connecting, inviting your heart to guide

Practice being with you, allowing who you truly are to unfold

Practice without resisting, you allow the flow like a song

The power of the pause...granting yourself "Being"

Allowing the flow like a song is freeing!

Embody the dance of the heart and mind your heart knows all
Your mind listens, your body resonates. Listen listen deeply

Return to the wisdom of the heart of a human
Your life will thank you for it every time.

EMBRACE GRACE
By: *Selma Harwell*

Born anew as we embrace grace Bliss bless effortless Bliss bless limitless. Grace - A true moment you sense inside Curiously in wonder, not knowing why. Embrace is like melting into earth mother's arms Her healing touch spreads her wellness charms Earth mama's arms reach out to the sky Because she's made of energy-that's why! Just like you and just like me Bliss bless effortless

Just like a mother she calls to us "Clean up your mess And restore the rainforests We need space to chase For the fun of the run The better we breathe, The more expansion" Bliss bless clean your mess

Earth's forests The lungs of our world Keeping our air clean for us, Forests for us! Hold space for that beauty That has ever been, Deeply deeply breathing it in Bliss bless Limitless

Imagine those rainforests renewed To the way they once grew The lungs of the earth rescued - The way that it was. Hold that picture clearly of what Mother earth brought to us. Hold the space of beauty That has ever been. Deeply deeply breathe it in Bliss bless clean your mess Let's restore the forest As we've been taught Our courage is needed To fill up our heart, Bliss bless clean our mess Bliss bless Effortless. Loving me is Loving you. Playful and free

Practice becomes skill that strengthens your will. Strengthen your will along with kindness , the power of both shows up our blindness. Bliss bless limitless . Natural expression brings intentional joy Practicing intention has the magic of a toy That develops into miracles! Oh boy! More miracles please Bliss bless limitless Embrace grace of mind journey to The rainforest No separation. Bliss bless Limitless

POET: Jessica Louise Phillips

WHAT WOULD LOVE DO?

Love would have me believe I am worthy.
Love would guide me to happiness.
Love would redirect me to alignment.
Love would trust before the next steps have been revealed.
Love would understand that with great love can come great hurt and loss, and that it's all truly beautiful.
Love would cry for me, for you, for all of us.

Love would be patient, not just with self and others, but in those periods of separation and the unknown.
Love would bring me back to myself in those voids and moments in-between.

Love would be gracious in honoring and accepting others' decisions made in love, even when it hurts.
Love would cherish precious moments in the past knowing their depth will forever remain true.
Love would remember that it transcends all of time and space, and that time really means nothing.
Love would feel solace in the memory that we'll all reunite in the stars one day.
Love would never push away, or perhaps some days it would.
Love would do what it could and then lean into sweet surrender.
Love would consider what of this I'm experiencing is mine, and what is yours?
Love would realize that with a great capacity to love comes an even greater capacity to grieve.
Love would guide me to believe deep down that it's always worth it.
Love would know that my tears are your tears, your tears are my tears, and that all tears are our tears.
Love would tell me I'm ready and brave for feeling it all.
Love would feel the feelings and then make a choice to go where the love is.
Love would trust the bigger picture.
Love would keep whispering, 'It will all make sense one day.'
Love would remember that we are all separate, yet all one.
Love would know that we are all different, yet all the same.
Love would always find a way. Even if it's not the one I originally planned or hoped for.
Love would continue to remind me that 'That which is meant for me won't ever pass me by.'
Love would claim 'If not this, something even better.'
Love would remind me, 'I'm exactly where I'm meant to be, doing

exactly what I'm meant to be doing, with exactly who I'm meant to be with right now', even if that's just me, myself & I.
Love would direct me to deeply love, forgive and accept myself.
Love would remember that sleep and laughter are two of the best medicines.
Love would encourage me to keep being a warrior of light in this world.
Love would notify me everyday that our true purpose is to enjoy life and love others.
Love would insist I love myself first and give from a full cup.
Love would keep going.
Love would keep leading.
Love would keep paving the way.
Love will prevail.
Love will remain.
Love is here.
Love is you.
Love is me.
Love is.

BACK TO THE BREATH
By: *Jessica Louise Phillips*

The more I open my heart,
The more the mind seems to expand and fill with doubts.
The doubts, the fears, the triggers.

Back to the breath.
Back to the body.
Back to the breath.
Back to the body.

Except this time the mind is still going.
Still whirring and stirring
Still revving and choking and smoking.

Surely it will implode or self-combust soon?!
Then the lights will go out and the sound will switch off.

The only guaranteed place of peace at the moment is in sleep.
Nature the only other solace.
An ocean view and the sound of the waves.
As I lay crying, feeling, alchemising.

This too shall pass, I know.
But right now it hurts, it hurts, it hurts.

Reminding myself that the other side of this is going to feel...

Well, something beyond anything I'm able to fully comprehend right now.

There is so much going on behind the scenes that we can not see.
Trust.
Lean into the mystery.
For it will all make sense one day.

I HEAR YOU THE LOUDEST
By: *Jessica Louise Phillips*

What will it take?...
For people to slow down.
For people to not rush.
For people to listen.
For people to not interrupt.
For people to pause.
For people to tune in.
For people to be aware of their surroundings.
For people to consider others.
(For people to consider me!)

For people to not push or shove others out of the way.
For people to hold space.
For people to hear.
For people to know when to step back and when to lean in.
For people to not judge or project.
For people to drop the hierarchy.

"Don't let them silence you." Yes, but please be quieter.
My head and heart and nervous system need a break!
"You're not too much." Yes, but sometimes you're too loud.
For me.
You don't need to stomp and shout to be heard. To be important.
To be of value.
You don't need to be the loudest or boldest in the room to matter
in this world.

Everyone is a mirror and I'm aware I myself hold the keys to this question.
Yet I'll never forget when a kindred spirit found my eyes post-breathwork in a noisy bell tent.
She came to me in silence, held my hands and whispered,
"I hear you the loudest."

AND MY HEART OVERFLOWS
By: *Jessica Louise Phillips*

And my heart overflows
Knowing I get to go
To far off places
Whenever I please.

To connect with ancient lands
Uncovering untold secrets, within and without
Immersing in worlds
In ways I never could within the four walls of home.

Meeting souls, old and new
Experiencing heartache
And the spectrum of emotions
Grieving what's mine and what's not.

Connecting to lost parts of myself
Feeling it all
Embracing the elements
Surviving, thriving, living life.

Making sense through the stars
Wearing multiple scars
Laughing at the polarities
And the things that make no sense, just yet.

Either way,
Thankful
Grateful
Blessed.

POET: Sabrina L. Avalo

LIFE REVISE

I never knew that pain could be long lasting,

Shattered my heart to a million pieces, "Air grasping"!!

I close my eyes in disbelief, could it be true, the words she speaks?

Afraid to open my eyes, for with words I've lost life, self meaning, is that you lord that deceives me?
I gave my all to you, so why does this news make me blue ?
Enraged, ready to catch a case, Lord calm me down, give me strength!

I hear it over and over, I'm crying my eyes out, am I sober ??

Is this a dream, a movie scene? Wake me up, wake me out of this please.

I feel the black cloud darkening my mind, I'm asking you lord,
Take one more angel, one whose heart can't find...
find the strength to achieve letting go of what I don't want to believe.

I have the bullet with me, I'm losing me...

Im back, sorry I lost myself, for a sudden moment couldn't grasp mental health
the demon took over me, my angels kept fighting, to clear my mind of the Devil's confinement.

The lord slowed me down, from my frantic thinking, I remember who I am now, so soft and dreamy.
Standing strong in love and all that I achieve in. I was lost but now found, I am something to believe in.
Turned a frown to a smile, once shattered heart, now just bruises.
I took control of myself, now there's no losing.
Tried to bring me down, but look who's pursuing, Baby I'm a firework,
Protector of my doing.
-Svalo

POET: Kari Russell

YES

you said yes
not because you knew
but because you trusted

you said yes
not because it was logical
but because it felt euphoric

you said yes
not because it was trendy
but because it was unconventional

you said yes

not because it was proven to work
but because you knew you'd be ok if it didn't

you said yes
not because it made sense
but because it didn't

you said yes
not because you didn't feel fear
but because you did

yes...you said yes

POET: Aros Crystos

CHANNELING DOLPHINS

In the sea where we swim, we guide you to be free,
To experience the song of your heart, a divine start to be.
To live in the present is your life's true essence.
In the ocean's dance of bliss, we serenade you with a divine kiss.
Beloved one, recall the divine song within your being,
As our sounds and vibrations change humanity's seeing.
Recognize your own divine face,
For your voice is a treasure of grace.
In that sound, what can be found?
Portals leading humans out of the maze,
Into realms of grace where light endlessly plays.
As written in the lore of old, your beloved soul, ancient and bold,

Fulfills a divine goal, a light so bright,
Inspiring people to see and long for freedom's flight.

POET: BLESILDA CARMONA DE LA ROSA

BALLAD OF INTENT
(For my husband, Leandro)

Fire and Earth: they say we wouldn't mesh.
Fire and Dragon: they say we're enemies,
yet your Moon in Eagle-Phoenix and my Moon in Star-Twin-Fish
could
be proof that we can coexist
as long as we can turn roadblocks into Rainbows
for our love to light our bliss;
and blessed that we are, Angels of Earth and Fire,
we know that we're bright-invincible in such
a Time and Space as this.
Ergo: Love is a boundless miracle between the two of us.

ABOUT: Radhaa Publishing House

BECOME AN AUTHOR
BECOME A CONTRIBUTING WRITER

Radhaa Publishing House is a holistic publishing company that focuses on helping heart-centered, mind-expanding, truth-telling authors get their work out into the world. Our focus is on collaborative book series and memoirs. We thrive on supporting our authors and contributing writers throughout this journey, empowering them to step into their divine and an authentic voice while sharing their truth with the world. We especially celebrate cultural diversity worldwide, and we believe in weaving international voices to come together.

HOW ARE WE DIFFERENT?

Many collaborative publishing companies bundle the authors together so that they don't receive individual credit and acknowledgment. We make sure each Author is seen and heard and can be found easily. This has led to authors telling us that they have received more traffic and business and clients on their websites. In a sense, each of the Book we create is also like a Directory highlighting contributing writers unique offerings. This has been a win-win for the contributing writers and authors.

Here is what our authors have said about working with us:

"I felt totally supported. The best bit was feeling like being part of a loving family who wants you to be your best, do your best, and is there for you every step of the way. It also boosted my confidence as a writer. The collaborative nature of the project also made it way more fun than doing things alone".
- ***Arrameia, Prague***

"Visibility was a big piece of me coming out of the spiritual closet, and I felt that Radhaa Publishing House has a high energy and integrity level. Both of which are important for light workers and Starseeds. The curators and authors are light workers. Radhaa Publishing House created this wonderful opportunity for many others to be a part of. I felt that they put their whole heart into making this happen even before, during, and after the book is published. It was a project that was totally supportive that made me feel safe to share myself and my story." - ***Lalitah, Turkey***

"It was wonderful to work with Radhaa Publishing House. I saw the effort and perseverance the whole team has and the support system they have for all the authors. I have matured as an author from this experience. I was so inspired after writing my chapter in this book,

Awakening Starseeds, that I wrote an entire book called The Great Awakening because I was deeply moved writing."
   - Leshara, Philippines

"My story was edited by Radhaa Publishing House, and let me tell you, it put me in tears! They made it better than the way I originally wrote and submitted it while keeping my story and voice true to its events. I read it, and tears just flowed because it was so good!"- **Cristal, Florida**

"I have published many books on Consciousness, empowerment subjects, and relationships, but I had never revealed raw, real stories of my life as with Awakening Starseeds. I wanted to join other authors writing personal stories, and Radhaa Publishing House made it simple and empowering to share from my heart in a real, raw way. This team of conscious, awesome Starseeds encourages a revolution to Awaken other Starseeds worldwide!" - **Stasia, Utah**

This is an opportunity to STEP OUT, SPEAK OUR TRUTHS. This is our time, an obligation to share and support others that live in fear and question their soul paths, their soul journey. - **Breda, Canada**

At **Radhaa Publishing House,** we are highly involved in the entire process and work personally with the authors to navigate authorship challenges.

Our authors are heart-centered, soul-driven, and ready to manifest their legacy. We acknowledge the courage and strength it takes to step out into the public eye, and our team is here to support you all the way.

Creating a book is a tedious process and requires persistence, patience, and perspective. There are many moving parts of the book that need attention, and our team knows how to work hard to ensure we can come through with flying colors for the final date of our release.

Step into your voice and be heard now! When you become a contributing writer or an author of Radhaa Publishing House, you empower yourself in a way you may have never experienced before. That's what our authors tell us. Claim your author power now!

"Be that change you wanted to be in our world!"

If you have a compelling story to share with the world, dream of being a published author, and wish to be a part of the Radhaa Publishing family, reach out to us.

"No other publishing company offers you in-house support the way that Radhaa Publishing House does. Your legacy awaits!"

To find out more information about how to Join us, Become an Author or See our Upcoming Books, please visit our Website at:
www.RadhaaPublishingHouse.com
Email: RadhaaPublishing@gmail.com

You Make a Difference When You Support Our Holistic Books!

Published Books:

Awakening Starseeds: Shattering Illusions, Vol.1
Awakening Starseeds: Stories Beyond The Stargate, Vol. 2
Awakening Starseeds: Dreaming into the Future, Vol. 3
Pillars of Light: Stories of Goddess Activations™
Energy Healing & Soul Medicine
Stories of the Goddess: Divine Feminine Frequency Keepers
Quan Yin Goddess Activations™ Healing Workbook
Dolphin Odyssey
Infinite Cosmic Records: Sacred Doorways to Healing & Remembering
Poems From The Heart

To Order a Signed Copies of our Books, visit our Online Store: https://radhaanilia.net/shop/
Email us: RadhaaPublishing@gmail.com

Thank you for your support!

Special Message to Our Readers

*D*ear Readers,

Thank you for joining us on this heartfelt journey through **POEMS FROM THE HEART**. Your presence here signifies a deep connection and shared experience that we cherish.

If any poems resonate with you, please consider leaving a review for the poets on Amazon. Your words can have a profound impact. Here are some questions to guide your review:

- Which poem touched your soul the most and why?
- How did the themes of the book echo your journey?
- Did the poetry stir new emotions or insights within you?
- Would you share this book with others, and if so, why?

Your feedback is a treasured gift that helps our poets continue to share their voices. Supporting our small publishing house and exploring our other books means more to us than words can express.

Together we RISE!
With Love,
Radhaa of Radhaa Publishing House Team

If you like our book

POEMS FROM THE HEART

Please support us by leaving a review.

REVIEW us ONLINE at: Amazon.com.

We cannot do this without your support! Share our journey with others! With Love and Gratitude!
Thank you!